Passing the Numeracy Skills Test

Third edition

Mark Patmore

LearningMatters

First edition published in 2000 by Learning Matters Ltd.
Second edition published in 2001. Reprinted twice in 2001. Reprinted in 2002.
Third edition published in 2003. Reprinted in 2004 (twice). Reprinted in 2005.

© Mark Patmore

British Library Cataloguing in Publication Data
A CIP record for this book is available from the British Library.

ISBN 1 903300 94 0

Learning Matters Ltd
33 Southernhay East
Exeter EX1 1NX
Tel: 01392 215560
Email: info@learningmatters.co.uk
www.learningmatters.co.uk

Cover Design by Topics – The Creative Partnership
Text design by Code 5 Design Associates Ltd
Project Management by Deer Park Productions
Typeset by Mathematical Composition Setters Ltd, Salisbury, Wiltshire
Printed and bound in Great Britain by Cromwell Press, Trowbridge, Wiltshire

Contents

The QTS skills tests

If you wish to obtain Qualified Teacher Status (QTS) you will need to pass three online skills tests before being awarded QTS and beginning your induction period. The tests must be taken by all new entrants into the teaching profession regardless of training route, including those training in School Centred Initial Teacher Training and on the Graduate and Registered Teacher Programmes (GRTP).

The three tests cover skills in:

- **numeracy;**
- **literacy;**
- **information and communication technology (ICT).**

The tests will demonstrate that you can apply these skills to the degree necessary for their use in your day-to-day work in a school, rather than the subject knowledge required for teaching. The tests are taken online by booking a time at a specified centre, are marked instantly and your result, along with feedback on that result, will be given to you before you leave the centre.

You will find more information about the skills tests and the specified centres on the Teacher Training Agency (TTA) website: *www.canteach.gov.uk.*

Titles in this series

This series of books is designed to help you become familiar with the skills you will need to pass the tests and to practise questions on each of the topic areas to be tested.

Passing the Numeracy Skills Test (third edition)
Mark Patmore
ISBN 1 903300 94 0

Passing the Literacy Skills Test
Jim Johnson
ISBN 1 903300 12 6

Passing the ICT Skills Test
Clive Ferrigan
ISBN 1 903300 13 4

To order, please contact our distributors:
BEBC Distribution, Albion Close, Parkstone, Poole, BH12 3LL
Tel: 0845 230 9000 Email: learningmatters@bebc.co.uk

Check out our free online practice numeracy and literacy skills tests at
www.learningmatters.co.uk/education/

Introduction to the test

The numeracy skills test will have two sections:

→ *section 1 for the 'mental arithmetic' questions;*

→ *and section 2 for the 'written' questions, known as 'on-screen' questions*

In the mental arithmetic section calculators will not be allowed but noting numbers, jotting down working will be permitted. A 'drop-down' on-screen calculator will be provided for working through the 'on-screen' questions.

Each of the mental arithmetic questions will have a fixed time in which you must answer but there will be a total time available for you to answer all the on-screen questions. The on-screen questions will comprise a number of:

- **multiple choice questions where you will choose the correct response to a question from a number of possible responses;**
- **multiple response questions where you will have to choose more than one correct response from a number of possible answers;**
- **questions requiring a single response;**
- **questions where you will have to 'point and click' on the correct response;**
- **questions where you will 'drag and drop' your chosen answer onto selected boxes.**

The contexts for the questions

One of the aims of the numeracy skills test is to ensure that teachers have the skills and understanding necessary to analyse the sort of data that is now available in schools and consequently most questions will be set within contexts such as:

- **national test data;**
- **target setting and school improvement;**
- **the day-to-day analysis that takes place within schools – free school meals, pupil progress, costings, budgets, planning trips; etc.**

The following notes provide an indication of the sort of data that is available to help in the analysis of a school's performance and how it might be used.

Percentage of all pupils achieving each level in the 2002 Key Stage 2 Tests and Teacher Assessments in English, mathematics and science.

example

English	D	A	B	N	W	1	2	3	4	5	6	4+
Test	1	1	3	2	—	—	1	17	46	29	0	75
Reading	1	1	3	4	—	—	—	12	42	38	—	80
Writing	1	1	3	4	—	—	—	31	43	17	—	60
Teacher Assessment	0	0	—	—	1	1	5	21	49	24	0	73
Mathematics	**D**	**A**	**B**	**N**	**W**	**1**	**2**	**3**	**4**	**5**	**6**	**4+**
Test	0	1	2	2	—	—	1	20	46	27	0	73
Teacher Assessment	0	0	—	—	1	1	4	20	47	26	1	74
Science	**D**	**A**	**B**	**N**	**W**	**1**	**2**	**3**	**4**	**5**	**6**	**4+**
Test	0	2	1	0	—	—	0	9	49	38	0	86
Teacher Assessment	0	0	—	—	0	0	2	14	52	30	0	82

Note:

D represents pupils who have been disapplied.
A represents pupils who have failed to register a level due to absence.
B represents pupils who were assessed by teacher assessment only.
N represents pupils who took the tests but failed to register a level.
W represents pupils who are working towards level 1.

Clearly it is possible to see that the number of pupils who gained a level 4 or more in mathematics in the tests was 73% (46% + 27% + 0%). A school which had, for example, only 67% of its pupils gaining a level 4 or above was clearly performing below the national average in mathematics. However, for school results in English and science of 85% and 93% respectively, different conclusions could be drawn.

Percentage of pupils attaining level 4 or above in:

	National test results	School results	Difference in percentage points
Mathematics	73	67	−6
English (Reading)	80	85	+5
Science	86	93	+7

The school clearly performed better in science than in English. Tables like these can be produced for successive years and you might be asked to compare progress in a school or in a subject over a period of time.

This analysis can be refined by considering the performance in each subject for the lower, and upper quartiles and the median. Quartiles are explained below.

Upper Quartile (UQ) – the score or level for which 25% of the relevant pupils or schools achieved a higher result.

Median – the score or level for which 50% of the relevant pupils or schools achieved a higher result.

Lower Quartile (LQ) – the score or level for which 25% of the relevant pupils or schools achieved a lower result.

The quartile table showing the percentages of 11-year-olds in schools in England achieving a level 4 or above in English, mathematics and science is as follows:

Quartiles for test results			
	Upper quartiles	Median	Lower quartiles
English	87	78	66
Mathematics	86	76	64
Science	96	90	81

This table shows, for example, that the median percentage of 11-year-olds in each school achieving level 4 or above in mathematics was 76% and that schools in the top quarter had 86% or more pupils at level 4 or above and schools in the bottom quarter had 64% or fewer pupils at level 4.

The performance of a school with 67% of its pupils gaining level 4 in mathematics is roughly between the lower quartile and the median value.

Benchmarking

The benchmark information provided for schools is shown in the Autumn Package for different per-centage bands of free school meals. The bands are:

- up to and including 8% eligible for free school meals;
- more than 8% and up to 20% eligible for free school meals;
- more than 20% and up to 35% eligible for free school meals;
- more than 35% and up to 50% eligible for free school meals;
- more than 50%.

Benchmark tables indicate performance at various points in a distribution. These are:

95th percentile, UQ, 60th percentile, Median, 40th percentile, LQ, 5th percentile

usually labelled as 95%, UQ, 60%, Median, 40%, LQ, 5%.

The following illustration explains percentiles: the 40th percentile is the score or level for which 40% of the relevant pupils or schools achieved a lower level.

For example, primary school tables are produced showing performance in the core subjects at level 4 and above, at level 5 and above and the average level for each band. These tables enable a school to compare its performance with schools that are similar. There are equivalent tables for secondary schools.

A junior school with 18% of its pupils eligible for free school meals would use the appropriate table for the 8% to 20% band showing the percentage of pupils achieving level 4 and above in the Key Stage 2 statutory tests.

	95%	UQ	60%	Median	40%	LQ	5%
English	94	85	80	77	75	69	56
Mathematics	95	84	79	76	73	67	52
Science	100	95	92	90	88	83	70

If only 68% of the eligible pupils achieved level 4 or above in mathematics, a school's performance would be only just above the lower quartile for similar schools.

National value added information

The information provided here will enable a school to compare the progress made by an individual pupil in the school with the progress made by pupils nationally between e.g. Key Stage 1 and Key Stage 2, or Key Stage 2 and Key Stage 3. i.e. 'value added information'.

For these analyses the levels awarded are converted into points. The table below shows the points score equivalences that have been used at Key Stage 2.

This table, (there is a similar one for the Secondary phase), could be used to calculate:

Level	Points	Level	Points
Absent (A)	Disregard	Level 2	15
Disapplied (D)	Disregard	Level 3	21
Fail to achieve a level (N)	15	Level 4	27
Teacher Assessment (B)	15	Level 5	33
		Level 6	39

(i) the average points score for a pupil – defined as the points gained averaged over the core subjects.

A pupil awarded levels 5, 4 and 5 in English, mathematics and science respectively would gain an average points score of:

$$\frac{3\dot{3} + 27 + 33}{3} = 31$$

(If s/he were absent for the science test the average points score would be $\frac{33 + 27}{2} = 30$)

(ii)   the average points score for a school for a subject.

A school with 100 eligible pupils who, in English say, gained levels 5, 5, 3, 4, 5, 5, 2, 4, ... would have an average points score of:

$$\frac{33 + 33 + 21 + 27 + 33 + 33 + 15 + 27 + ...}{100}$$

Average points scores can be used to compare progress across Key Stages:

The graph below indicates the value added line relating pupils' average performance in their Key Stage 2 tests with that achieved 3 years later at Key Stage 3.

Key Stage 3 Average Test Level Median Line

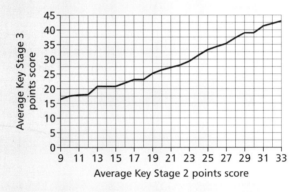

This graph suggests that an average points score of 19 at Key Stage 2 would give a points score of about 25 at Key Stage 3.

A different form of comparison that has been used are 'chances' graphs which are produced for a range of point scores from the previous Key Stage for different subjects.

Key Stage 2 Average Points Score <22

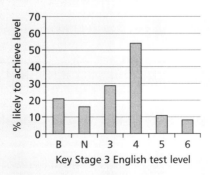

If a pupil gains a Key Stage 2 average points score of 21 then, for English, the chart suggests that such a pupil has about an 11% likelihood of gaining a level 5 at Key Stage 3.

Mathematical areas

The numeracy test will include questions covering the range of contexts and types of responses within 3 areas:

1　Carrying out calculations using mental arithmetic.
2　Using and applying general arithmetic.
3　Interpreting and using statistical information.

Note that inevitably there will be a degree of overlap between these areas.

Carrying out calculations using mental arithmetic

These questions are intended to ensure an acceptable level of mental agility, and to check that you are able to use and apply numerical information. The questions will require you to complete mental calculations of more than one stage, involving, for example: time; money; fractions, decimals, percentage and proportion; measurement; conversion (e.g. converting between currencies or converting between fractions, decimals and percentages); and combinations of one or more of the four rules of arithmetic. Calculators will not be permitted, but you will be able to jot down any workings.

Using and applying general arithmetic

The questions in this section will require you to use and apply basic arithmetic processes correctly using: time; money; fractions, decimals, percentage, ratio and proportion; measurement, e.g., distance, area; conversion (e.g., converting between currencies or converting between fractions, decimals and percentages); average (i.e. mean, median and mode); simple formulae.

Interpreting and using statistical information

This section will require you to demonstrate that you can:

- **identify trends correctly;**
- **make comparisons in order to draw conclusions;**
- **interpret information accurately.**

Basic structure of the book

The book is divided into sections:

Section I: a very short section included to remind you of the basic arithmetic processes. The majority of you will be able to miss this unit out but some may find a need to revise fractions, decimals and percentages, etc.

Sections 2 to 4 inclusive: cover the three 'content' areas (see above), one area per section.

Section 5: answers and key points.

In each section the additional required knowledge, language and vocabulary are explained and worked examples of the type of questions to be faced are provided together with the practice questions. The answers for these questions are given at the end of the book, together with further advice and guidance on solutions.

Fractions, decimals and percentages

You must remember decimals and place value:

hundreds	tens	ones	.	tenths	hundredths
4	3	5	•	2	7

4 hundreds + 3 tens + 5 ones + 2 tenths + 7 hundredths

$$= 400 + 30 + 5 + \frac{2}{10} + \frac{7}{100}$$

$$= 435.27$$

Take care when adding or subtracting decimals to line up the decimal points. Remember, too, when multiplying decimals by 10 that all the digits move one place to the left, so 435.27×10 becomes 4352.7, and when dividing by 100 the digits move two places to the right so $4352.7 \div 100$ becomes 43.527.

When multiplying two decimals the method you may remember is to 'ignore' the decimal points, do the multiplication and then count up the number of decimal figures in the question numbers – the total will give the number of decimal figures in the answer number, so that 0.4×0.5 is calculated as $4 \times 5 = 20$; there are 2 decimal figures in the question (numbers 4 and 5) so there are 2 in the answer. Therefore the answer is 0.20. It would be better to think of this calculation as follows:

$$0.4 \times 0.5 = \frac{4}{10} \times \frac{5}{10} = \frac{20}{100} = 0.2$$

You must remember how to work with fractions. There are several ways of 'looking' at a fraction, for example: $\frac{3}{4} = 3$ parts out of 4; or 3 divided by 4; or 3 shared by $4 = 3 \div 4 = 0.75$; or three lots of a quarter $= 3 \times \frac{1}{4}$; or a quarter of $3 = \frac{1}{4} \times 3$.

One way to calculate, say, $\frac{2}{5}$ of £20 is: find a fifth, £20 ÷ 5 = £4 then multiply this by 2 = £8. Another way is to change the fraction into a decimal:

$\frac{2}{5} = 2 \div 5 = 0.4$, then multiply $0.4 \times £20 = £8$.

You will need to know how to simplify a fraction by dividing both the numerator and the denominator by the same factor.

$\frac{12}{28} = \frac{3}{7}$ dividing the numerator and the denominator by 4	*example*

or $\frac{54}{72} = \frac{27}{36} = \frac{9}{12} = \frac{3}{4}$ dividing top and bottom by 2 then by 3 and then by 3 again.

You must remember that percentages are fractions with denominators of 100 (per cent means per 100). For example, 5% represents $\frac{5}{100}$, 75% represents $\frac{75}{100}$.

You can convert percentages to decimals by dividing by 100, so 5% = $\frac{5}{100}$ = 0.05, and 75% = $\frac{75}{100}$ = 0.75.

To change a fraction into a percentage first change it into a decimal and then multiply by 100.

$\frac{3}{8}$ as a percentage is 3 ÷ 8 = 0.375 × 100 = 37.5%   ***example***

To find the percentage of a quantity change the % into a decimal and then multiply the result by the quantity.

example

either find 30% of 50 = 0.3 × 50 = 15.

or find 10% of 50 = $\frac{1}{10}$ × 50 = 5 so 30% = 3 × 10% = 3 × 5 = 15

You need to be able to calculate percentages in problems such as 'what is 14 marks out of 25 as a percentage?':

example

either 14 out of 25 as a fraction is $\frac{14}{25}$ = $\frac{14}{25}$ × 100 = 14 × 4 = 56%

or use equivalent fractions: $\frac{14}{25}$ = $\frac{56}{100}$ (multiplying by 4 to get a denominator of 100)
                                                        = 56%

Percentages are useful for comparisons:

example

In a test Richard got 40 right out of 80, Sarah got 45% and Paul managed to get $\frac{5}{8}$ correct. Who did best and who did worst in the test?

Richard got 50%; Paul got $\frac{5}{8}$ × 100 = 62.5%

So Sarah did the worst and Paul did the best.

Here are some common fractions, decimals and percentages.
You should learn these.

1%	=	$\frac{1}{100}$	=	0.01	(divide by 100)
5%	=	$\frac{1}{20}$	=	0.05	(divide by 20)
10%	=	$\frac{1}{10}$	=	0.1	(divide by 10)
$12\frac{1}{2}$%	=	$\frac{1}{8}$	=	0.125	(divide by 8)
20%	=	$\frac{1}{5}$	=	0.2	(divide by 5)
25%	=	$\frac{1}{4}$	=	0.25	(divide by 4)
50%	=	$\frac{1}{2}$	=	0.5	(divide by 2)
75%	=	$\frac{3}{4}$	=	0.75	(divide by 4, multiply by 3)

questions

1 Calculate these totals without using a calculator:

(a) $1.8 + 2.0 + 0.5$ (b) $0.4 + 0.04 + 4$ (c) $2.1 + 0.09 + 7 + 0.9$

(d) $2.8 + 3.2 - 0.6$ (e) $0.04 + 1.04 + 0.4$ (f) $2.01 + 0.09 + 7 + 0.09$

2 Calculate these without using a calculator:

(a) 1.4×30 (b) 0.5×0.7 (c) 0.4×5

3 Write these percentages as fractions in their simplest form:

(a) 2% (b) 25% (c) 85% (d) 12.5% (e) 47%

4 Write these fractions as percentages:

(a) $\frac{3}{8}$ (b) $\frac{13}{25}$ (c) $\frac{12}{40}$ (d) $\frac{36}{60}$

5 Work these out:

(a) 25% of £40   (b) 75% of £20   (c) 12% of 50   (d) 20% of 45

6 Simplify these fractions, writing them in their lowest terms:

(a) $\frac{24}{36}$ (b) $\frac{18}{30}$ (c) $\frac{30}{75}$ (d) $\frac{75}{100}$

7 Which is largest?

$\frac{90}{150},\ \frac{39}{60},\ \frac{61}{100}$

Mean, median, mode and range

The *mean* is the average most people give if asked for an average – the mean is found by adding up all the values in the list and dividing this total by the number of values.

The *median* is the middle value when all the values in the list are put in size order. If there are two 'middle' values the median is the mean of these two.

The *mode* is the most common value.

The *range* is the difference between the highest value and the lowest value.

This example should illustrate the calculations:

The children in Class 6 gained the following marks in a test:

Boys:	45	46	48	60	42	53	47	51
	54	54	49	48	47	53	48	45

Girls:	45	47	47	55	46	53	54	63
	48	50	46	51	48	48		

Work out the mean, median, mode and range for the boys and girls and compare the distributions of the marks.

The calculation for the boys:

$$\text{Mean: } \frac{42 + 45 + 45 + 46 + 47 + 47 + 48 + 48 + 48 + 49 + 51 + 53 + 53 + 54 + 54 + 60}{16}$$

$$= 49 \text{ (to the nearest whole number)}$$

Median: there are 16 values, so the median is midway between the 8th and 9th values $= \frac{48 + 48}{2} = 48$.

The *mode* is 48.

The *range* is $60 - 42 = 18$.

8

Now work out the values for the girls.

question

Notes

The mathematics required in this part of the test should usually be straightforward. The content and skills likely to be tested are listed in the Introduction (see page 1). Look back at this to remind yourself.

> **Key Point**
> *When you are taking the test, listen for, and jot down, numbers that may give short cuts or ease the calculations, such as those that allow doubling and halving. For example, multiply by 100 then divide by 2 if you need to multiply by 50, or multiply by 100 and divide by 4 if you are multiplying by 25. To calculate percentages, first find 10% by dividing by 10 then double for 20% or divide by 2 for 5% and so on.*

Remember:

- **Calculators are not allowed.**
- **Questions will be read out twice. When answering the questions in this section, ask someone to read each question out to you and then, without a pause, read out the question again.**
- **There should then be a pause to allow you to record the answer before the next question is read out. The pause should be 15 seconds long.**

questions

1. As part of a two and a quarter hour tennis training session pupils received specialist coaching for one hour and twenty minutes. How many minutes of the training session remained?

2. A test has forty questions, each worth one mark. The pass mark was seventy per cent. How many questions had to be answered correctly to pass the test?

3. Dining tables seat six children. How many tables are needed to seat one hundred children?

4. In a flu epidemic a quarter of the pupils in a school are ill. There are six hundred pupils in the school. How many are not ill?

5. A coach holds fifty-two passengers. How many coaches will be needed for a school party of four hundred and fifty people?

6. Eight kilometres is about five miles. About how many kilometres is thirty miles?

7. The journey from school to a sports centre took thirty-five minutes each way. The pupils spent two hours at the sports centre. They left school at 'o' nine thirty. At what time did they return?

8 It is possible to seat forty people in a row across the hall. How many rows are needed to seat four hundred and thirty-two people?

9 Pupils spent twenty five hours in lessons each week. Four hours per week were allocated to science. What percentage of the lesson time per week was spent on the other subjects?

10 A teacher wants to show a twenty-five-minute video. Tidying up the room and setting homework she estimates will take ten minutes. The lesson will finish at eleven forty-five. What is the latest time she can set the video to start?

11 In a test eighty per cent of the pupils in class A achieved level four and above. In class B twenty-two out of twenty-five pupils reached the same standard. What was the difference between the two classes in the percentage of pupils reaching level four and above?

12 Two hundred pupils correctly completed a sponsored spell of fifty words. Each pupil was sponsored at five pence per word. How much money did the pupils raise in total?

13 A pupil scores forty-two marks out of a possible seventy in a class test. What percentage score is this?

14 There are one hundred and twenty pupils in a year group. Each has to take home two notices. Paper costs three pence per copy. How much will the notices cost?

15 What is seven and a half per cent as a decimal?

16 In a class of thirty-five pupils, four out of seven are boys. How many girls are there in the class?

17 In a school there are five classes of twenty-five pupils and five classes of twenty-eight pupils. How many pupils are there in the school?

18 A school has four hours and twenty-five minutes class contact time per day. What is the weekly contact time?

19 The attendance rate in a school of three hundred children drops from ninety-six per cent to ninety-five per cent in consecutive weeks. How many more absences were there in the second week?

20 A teacher needs to interview forty pupils for their Record of Achievement. Each pupil is allocated eight minutes. What is the minimum number of half-hour lessons needed to carry out all of the interviews?

21 A teacher wants to record a film on a three-hour video tape which starts at eleven fifty-five p.m. and ends at one forty-five a.m. the following day. How much time will there be left on the tape?

22 A test has thirty questions, each worth one mark. If the pass mark is sixty per cent, what is the minimum number of questions that must be answered correctly in order to pass the test?

23 A space two point five metres by two point five metres is to be used for a flower bed. What is this area in square metres?

24 In a class of thirty pupils sixty per cent of the pupils are girls. How many boys are there in the class?

25 A school has nine hundred and fifty pupils on roll. Ninety per cent achieved full attendance. How many pupils were absent on at least one occasion?

26 Twenty per cent of the pupils in a school with three hundred and fifteen pupils have free school meals. How many pupils is this?

27 In a class of thirty-two pupils, three eighths are absent with flu. How many pupils are present?

28 A pupil scores fourteen out of a possible twenty-five in a test. What is this as a percentage?

29 Three fifths of a class of thirty-five pupils are boys. How many are girls?

30 A school's end of key stage mathematics test results for a class of twenty-five pupils showed that nineteen pupils achieved level five or above. What percentage was this?

31 What is twelve and one half per cent as a decimal?

32 What is four point zero five six multiplied by one hundred?

3 Using and applying general arithmetic

Notes

Many of the questions in the Skills Test will require you to be able to interpret charts, tables and graphs. These are usually straightforward but do make sure that you read the questions carefully and read the tables or graphs carefully so that you will be able to identify the correct information. These questions are so varied that it is difficult to give examples for all of them – practice makes perfect, though.

There are some questions for which you may wish to revise the mathematics:

Fractions and percentages

See the brief notes in the Basic Revision section 1, for the essential knowledge. If you have to calculate percentage increases (or decreases), the simplest method is: find the actual difference, divide by the original amount and then multiply by 100% to convert this fraction to a percentage.

> *example*
>
> *Last year 30 pupils gained a level 3 in the national assessment tests. This year 44 gained a level 3. Calculate the percentage increase.*
>
> Actual increase = 14.
> Percentage increase = $\frac{14}{30} \times 100\% = 46.667\%$

Rounding

Clearly this answer, 46.667%, is too accurate. It would be better written as 46.7% (written to 1 decimal place) or as 47% (to the nearest whole number). You need to be able to round answers to a given number of decimal places or to the nearest whole number (depending on what the question is demanding). The simple rule is that if the first digit that you wish to remove is 5 or more, then you add 1 to the last remaining digit in the answer. If the first digit is less than 5 then the digits are just removed.

Examples: 46.3   = 46 to the nearest whole number
           0.345   = 0.35 to 2 decimal places
        34.3478   = 34.348 to 3 decimal places
        34.3478   = 34.35 to 2 decimal places
        34.3478   = 34.3 to 1 decimal place
        34.3478   = 34 to the nearest whole number.

Ratio and proportion

These sorts of questions are best illustrated with examples:

(i) Divide £60 between 3 people in the ratio 1 : 2 : 3. The total number of 'parts' is 1 + 2 + 3 = 6.

example

> Therefore 1 part = £60 ÷ 6 = £10.
> Therefore the money is shared as £10; £20; £30.

(ii) Four times as many children in a class have school dinners as do not. If there are 30 children, how many have school dinners?

> The ratio 4 : 1 giving 4 + 1 = 5 parts. Therefore 1 'part' = 30 ÷ 5 = 6.
> Therefore 4 × 6 = 24 children have school dinners.

Don't confuse ratio and proportion. Ratio is 'part to part' while proportion is 'part to whole' and is usually given as a fraction. If the question had asked 'What proportion of children have school dinners?' the answer would be $\frac{24}{30} = \frac{4}{5}$.

Notes on measures

You need to know and be able to change between the main metric units of measurement. For example:

Length
    1 kilometre = 1000 metres
    1 metre = 100 centimetres or 1000 millimetres
    1 centimetre = 10 millimetres

Mass
    1 kilogram = 1000 grams
    1 tonne = 1000 kilograms

Capacity
    1 litre = 1000 millilitres = 100 centilitres

Notes on algebra

Generally a formula will be given to you, either in words or letters, and you will need to substitute numbers into that formula and arrive at an answer through what will be essentially an arithmetic rather than algebraic process. Remember the rules that tell you the order in which you should work through calculations:

→ **Brackets should be evaluated first.**

→ **Then work out the multiplications and divisions.**

→ **Finally work out the additions and subtractions.**

Thus: (i)   2 × 3 + 4 = 6 + 4 = 10 but 2 + 3 × 4 = 14 (i.e. 2 + 12) not 20.

        (ii) $\frac{6+4}{2} = \frac{10}{2} = 5$ not 3 + 4 = 7.

        (iii)   2(3 + 6) = 2 × 9 = 18.

<u>Note</u> that some of the questions that follow have several parts. In the actual test each 'part' would be a separate question, e.g. question 7 would be split into 4 different questions.

questions

1. There were 30 pupils in a class. Their results in a test are summarised in the table below.

Mark out of 40	Number of pupils achieving mark
33	2
29	5
34	5
36	7
19	2
24	8
27	1

What are the mean, mode and range for these results?

On the test this question could be a 'drag and drop' question as follows:

Place the correct values in the summary table below.

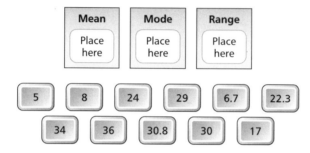

2. A teacher was planning a school trip to Germany. Each pupil was to be allowed 100 euros spending money. At the time she planned the trip £1 was equivalent to 1.43 euros. When the pupils went to Germany the exchange rate was £1 = 1.38 euros. How much more **English** money did each pupil have?

3. Five times as many pupils in a school obtained level 2 on the Key Stage 1 mathematics test as obtained level 3. If a total of 32 pupils took the test, and just 2 pupils obtained level 1, how many obtained level 3?

4. Teachers in a mathematics department analysed the Key Stage 2 national test results for mathematics from 3 feeder schools.

Level	School A Number of pupils	School B Number of pupils	School C Number of pupils	Totals
2	5	3	4	12
3	6	8	8	22
4	16	18	15	49
5	6	3	8	17
Totals	33	32	35	

Which school had the greatest percentage of pupils working at level 4 and above?

5 The national percentage of pupils with SEN (including statements) is about 18%. A school of 250 pupils has 35 children on the SEN register. How many is this below the national average?

6 For a GCSE subject, 20% of the final marks were allocated to coursework and 80% to the final examination. The coursework was marked out of 40 and the exam out of 200. A pupil scored 22 for coursework and 135 for the exam. What was the pupil's final percentage mark to the nearest whole number?

1   61%
2   62%
3   65%
4   66%

7 Year 10 students were asked to opt for either swimming or tennis. Their choices were:

	Swimming	Tennis
Girls	27	33
Boys	42	28

(a)   What was the total number of students who chose swimming?
(b)   What percentage of these were girls?
(c)   What percentage of the girls chose tennis?
(d)   What was the total percentage of students who chose swimming?

8 A pupil achieved a mark of 58 out of 75 for practical work and 65 out of 125 on the written paper. The practical mark was worth 60% of the final mark and the written paper 40% of the final mark. The minimum mark required for each grade is shown below.

Grade	Minimum mark
A*	80%
A	65%
B	55%
C	45%
D	35%

What was the grade achieved by this pupil?

9 A pupil obtained the following marks in three tests.
In which test did the pupil do best?

Test 1	Test 2	Test 3
$\frac{45}{60}$	$\frac{28}{40}$	$\frac{23}{30}$

10 The bar chart below shows the marks for a Year 7 test.

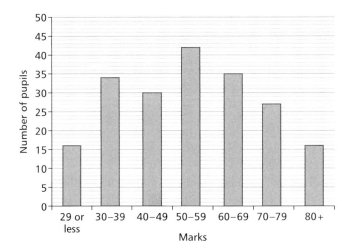

The pass mark for the test was 60 marks. What percentage of pupils passed the test?

11 This table shows the national benchmarks for level 4 and above at Key Stage 2:

Percentile	95th	Upper quartile	60th	40th	Lower quartile	5th
English	97	87	82	73	66	46
Mathematics	98	86	80	72	64	45
Science	100	96	93	87	81	63

Schools' results are placed into categories:

A* Within the top 5%.
A   Above the upper quartile and below the 95th percentile.
B   Above the 60th percentile and below the upper quartile.
C   Between the 40th and the 60th percentiles.
D   Below the 40th percentile and above the lower quartile.
E   Below the lower quartile and above the 5th percentile.
E* Below the 5th percentile.

What grades would be given for the core subjects in a school whose results were:

English	98%
Mathematics	85%
Science	83%

12 A teacher analysed pupil absence over a year and produced the following table:

Total number of half days of unauthorised absences each term

	Term 1	Term 2	Term 3	Total
Year 7	32	16	20	68
Year 8	28	31	30	89
Year 9	26	21	25	72
Year 10	32	21	31	84
Year 11	6	18	20	44
Total	124	107	126	

The school's target for the next year is to reduce the number of unauthorised absences by at least 5%. What will next year's target be, in half days? Give your answer to the nearest half day.

13 The levels gained in mathematics by the Year 6 pupils in a school in the national attainment tests are shown below. The results are given for Class 6A and 6B.

Level	Class 6A	Class 6B
N	1	3
2	2	3
3	11	7
4	11	14
5	5	1
6	0	0

(a) What percentage of the year group gained level 4 or above?

(b) Which class had the greater percentage gaining level 4 or above?

14 Four schools had the following proportion of pupils with special educational needs:

School	Proportion
P	$\frac{2}{9}$
Q	0.17
R	57 out of 300
S	18%

Which school had the lowest proportion of pupils with special needs?

(a) School P   (b) School Q   (c) School R   (d) School S

15 Table 1 shows the marks gained by a group of pupils in Year 3 in a mathematics test.

table 1

Pupil	Marks	Pupil	Marks
A	23	K	47
B	62	L	38
C	58	M	22
D	35	N	24
E	42	O	81
F	49	P	39
G	76	Q	65
H	80	R	71
I	23	S	73
J	62	T	25

The school will use the results to predict their levels for mathematics at the end of Year 6, and will target those pupils who, it is predicted, will miss level 4 by 1 level.

Table 2 is the conversion chart the school uses to change marks to expected levels.

table 2

Mark range	2–24	25–51	52–79	80 and over
Expected level	2	3	4	5

How many pupils will be targeted?

16 A school has analysed the results of its students at GCSE and A-level for several years and from these produced a graph which it uses to predict the average A-level points score for a given average points score at GCSE.

Use the graph below to predict the average points score at A-level if the GCSE points score were 6.

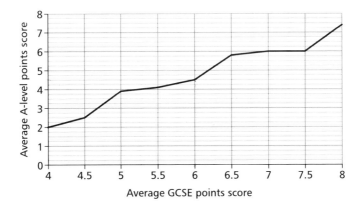

17 A junior school has a weekly lesson time of 23.5 hours. Curriculum analysis gives the following amount of time to the core subjects:

English:	6 hours 30 mins
Mathematics:	5 hours
Science:	1 hour 30 minutes.

Calculate the percentage of curriculum time given to English. Give your answer to the nearest per cent.

18 A support teacher assessed the reading ages of a group of 10 Year 8 pupils with Special Educational Needs.

Pupil	Actual age in		Reading age in	
	Years	Months	Years	Months
A	12	07	10	08
B	12	01	11	09
C	12	03	9	07
D	12	03	13	06
E	12	01	10	02
F	12	11	12	00
G	12	06	8	04
H	12	07	10	00
I	12	06	11	08
J	12	02	10	10

What percentage of the 10 pupils had a reading age of at least 1 year 6 months below the actual age?

19 A teacher analysed pupils' performance at the end of Year 5.
Pupils judged to have achieved level 3 and below were targeted for extra support.

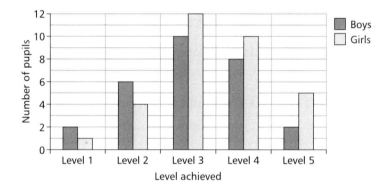

What fraction of the pupils needed extra support?

20 A plastic drinking cup has a capacity of 100 ml.
How many cups could be filled from a 1.5 litre carton of juice?

21 A teacher recorded the number of laps of a rectangular field walked by pupils in Years 5 and 6 in a school's annual walk for charity.

Year group	Number of pupils	Number of laps
5	65	8
6	94	10

The rectangular field measured 200 metres by 150 metres.
The teacher calculated the total distance covered.
Which of the following shows the total distance in kilometres?

(a) 1022   (b) 1460   (c) 10220   (d) 111.3

23

22 A primary teacher required each pupil to have a piece of card measuring 20 cm by 45 cm for a lesson. Large sheets of card measured 60 cm by 50 cm. What was the minimum number of large sheets of card required for a class of 28 pupils?

23 For a GCSE German oral examination 28 pupils had individual oral assessments with a language teacher.

Each individual assessment took 5 minutes. There was a changeover time of 2 minutes between each assessment.

A day was set aside for the assessments to take place with sessions that ran from 09:00 to 10:10, 10:45 to 11:55 and 13:15 to 15:00.

At what time did the last pupil finish?

(a) 14:09   (b) 14:00   (c) 13:43   (d) 13:45

24 The display area on the wall of a classroom is 2.5 metres by 1.5 metres.

What is its area in square metres?

25 Using the relationship 5 miles = 8 km, convert:
(a)   120 miles into kilometres.
(b)   50 km into miles.

(Give your answers to the nearest whole number in each case.)

26 A ream of photocopier paper is approximately 5 cm thick. What is the approximate thickness of 1 sheet of paper? Give your answers in millimetres.

27 A teacher helped a group of pupils to develop a rectangular environmental area in a school as part of the Healthy Schools campaign.

The dimensions of the area are shown below.

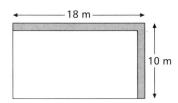

The pupils built a path around two sides using square paving slabs. Each slab measured 0.5 m × 0.5 m. The path was one slab wide.

How many paving slabs were needed to make the path?

28 A piece of fabric measuring 32 cm by 15 cm was required for each pupil in a Year 8 design and technology lesson. What was the minimum length of 120 cm wide fabric required for 29 pupils?

29 A school trip is organised from Derby to London – approximately 120 miles. A teacher makes the following assumptions:

(a)   The pupils will need a 30-minute break during the journey.
(b)   The coach will be able to average 40 miles an hour, allowing for roadworks and traffic.
(c)   The coach is due in London at 9 a.m.

What would be the latest time for the coach to leave Derby?

30 A teacher organised a hike for a group of pupils during a school's activity week. The route was measured on a 1 : 50000 scale map and the distances on the map for each stage of the hike were listed on the chart below:

	Stage of hike	Distance on map (cm)
1	Start to Stop A	14.3
2	Stop A to Stop B	8.7
3	Stop B to Stop C	9.3

What was the total distance travelled on the hike?
Give your answer to the nearest kilometre.

31 The following table shows the time for 4 children swimming in a relay race:

1st length	John	95.6 seconds
2nd length	Karen	87.3 seconds
3rd length	Julie	91.3 seconds
4th length	Robert	89.4 seconds.

What was the total time, in minutes and seconds, that they took?

32 A teacher completed the following expenses claim form after attending a training course:

	Travelling		
From	To	Miles	Expenses
School and return	Training centre to school	238	place here
Other expenses	Car parking		£7.50
	Evening meal		£10.50
		Total claim	place here

The mileage rates were:
   30p per mile for the first 100 miles
   26p per mile for the remainder.
Complete the claim form by placing the correct values in the expenses column.

   £40.88   £65.88   £71.38   £73.88   £83.88   £87.00   £89.40

33 A classroom assistant works from 9.00 a.m. until 12 noon for 4 days per week in a primary school and has a 15 minute break from 10.30 until 10.45. She provides learning support for pupils – each pupil receiving a continuous 20 minutes' session. How many pupils can she support each week?

34 A map has a scale of 1 cm to 6 km. A road on the map is measured as 7.2 cm long. How long is the road in kilometres?

35 A school is expecting 250 parents for a concert. Chairs are to be put out in rows in the hall. Each chair is 45 cm wide and chairs are fixed together in blocks of 8, two blocks making a row. There must be a gangway down the middle of the hall of 0.9 m between the blocks. How much space is needed for each row?

36 Equipment for a school is delivered in boxes 15 cm deep. The boxes are to be stacked in a cupboard which is 1.24 m high. How many layers of the boxes will fit into the cupboard?

37 A teacher arranged for four groups of pupils to try out a new interactive program on the classroom computer. He gave a 15-minute introduction and then each group in turn had 10 minutes working at the computer. The changeover time between groups was 2 minutes. How long did the session last?

38 A teacher planned a school trip from Calais to a study centre. The distance from Calais to the centre is 400 km. The coach is expected to travel at an average speed of 50 miles per hour, including time for breaks.

The coach is due to leave Calais at 06:20. What time should it arrive at the study centre?

Use the conversion rate of 1 km $= \frac{5}{8}$ mile.

Give your answer using the 24 hour clock.

39 In some GCSE examinations, coursework is marked by teachers in school and moderated by the examination board to ensure consistency. Teachers' marks may be brought 'into line' by applying a scaling rule. One example could be:

revised mark = teacher mark $\times$ 0.8 − 3.5.

What would be the revised mark of a candidate who was awarded 50 marks by a teacher?

40 Moderators sample the coursework marked by teachers in school. A moderator will select a sample from a school according to the guidelines and rules. One rule that fixes the size of the sample to be selected is:

Size (s) $= 10 + \dfrac{n}{10}$ where n is the number of candidates in a school.

What would be the sample size if there were 150 candidates?

41 The following formula converts degrees Fahrenheit (°F) into degrees Celsius (°C).

$$C = \frac{5(F-32)}{9}$$

Use this formula to change 180°F into Celsius.

42 Another formula is:

$$C = \left\{ \frac{5(F+40)}{9} \right\} - 40$$

Use this formula to change 68°F into degrees Celsius.

43 A pupil achieved the following scores in Tests A, B and C

Test	A	B	C
Actual mark	70	60	7

The pupil's weighted score was calculated using the following formula:

$$\text{Weighted score} = \frac{(A \times 60)}{100} + \frac{(B \times 30)}{80} + C$$

What was the pupil's weighted score?

Give your answer to the nearest whole number.

A teacher used a spreadsheet to calculate pupils' marks in a mock GCSE exam made up of two papers. Paper 1 was worth 25% of the total achieved and Paper 2 was worth 75% of the total achieved.

This table shows the first 4 entries in the spreadsheet:

	Paper 1 Mark out of 30	(25%) Weighted mark	Paper 2 Mark out of 120	(75%) Weighted mark	Final weighted mark
Pupil A	24	20	80	50	70
Pupil B	20	16.7	68	42.5	59.2
Pupil C	8	6.7	59	36.9	43.6
Pupil D	20	16.7	74	46.3	63

Pupil E scored 18 on Paper 1 and 64 on Paper 2.

What was the final weighted mark for Pupil E?

Give your answer to one decimal place.

 The table below shows the percentage test results for a group of pupils:

Pupils	Test 1	Test 2	Test 3	Test 4	Test 5	Test 6	Test 7	Test 8
A	92	85	87	82	78	26	92	95
B	53	70	72	38	15	27	83	73
C	61	77	69	68	60	30	90	77
D	95	100	93	30	92	30	100	70
E	72	49	47	42	46	82	72	92
F	58	78	38	46	34	58	98	78

Indicate all the true statements:

(a) the greatest range of % marks achieved was in Test 2
(b) Pupil C achieved a mean mark of 66.5%
(c) the median mark for Test 6 was 30.

 A single mark for GCSE coursework is calculated from three components using the following formula:

Final mark = Component A × 0.6 + Component B × 0.3 + Component C × 0.1.

A candidate obtained the following marks:

Component A   64
Component B   36
Component C   40

What was this candidate's final coursework mark?

A pupil submitted two GCSE coursework tasks, Task A and Task B.

Task A carried a weighting of 60% and Task B a weighting of 40%.

Each task was marked out of 100.

The pupil scored 80 marks in Task A.

What would be the minimum mark score required by the pupil in Task B to achieve an overall mark across the two tasks of 60%?

 A teacher set a pupil a target of achieving a mean score of 70% over four tests.

	Test 1 Out of 30	Test 2 Out of 30	Test 3 Out of 30	Test 4 Out of 30
Pupil	18	28	14	?

What was the lowest mark out of 30 that the pupil needed to achieve in Test 4 in order to achieve the target of an overall mean score of 70% that he was set?

 A teacher calculated the speed in kilometres per hour of a pupil who completed a 6 km cross country race.

Use the formula: Distance = speed × time.

The pupil took 48 minutes.

What was the pupil's speed in kilometres per hour?

 A readability test for worksheets, structured examination questions, etc. uses the formula:

$$\text{Reading level} = 5 + \left\{20 - \frac{x}{15}\right\}$$

Where x = the average number of monosyllabic words per 150 words of writing.

Calculate the reading level for a paper where $x = 20$.

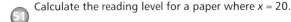 To help pupils set individual targets a teacher calculated predicted A level points scores using the following formula:

$$\text{Predicted A level points score} = \left(\frac{\text{total GCSE points score}}{\text{number of GCSEs}} \times 3.9\right) - 17.5$$

GCSE grades were awarded the following points:

GCSE grade	A^*	A	B	C
Points	8	7	6	5

Calculate the predicted A level points score for a pupil who at GCSE gained 4 passes at grade C, 4 at grade B, 1 at grade A and 1 at grade A^*.

 A candidate's final mark in a GCSE examination is calculated from two components as follows:

Final mark = mark in component 1 × 0.6 + mark in component 2 × 0.4.

A candidate needs a mark of 80 or more to be awarded a grade A^*. If the mark awarded in component 2 was 70, what would be the least mark needed in component 1 to gain a grade A^*?

53 Over a period of years a school has compared performance at GCSE with performance at Key Stage 3 and established rules for the core subjects which they use to predict GCSE grades. In order to do this they converted GCSE graded to points using the following table:

Grade	A^*	A	B	C	D	E	F	G
Points	8	7	6	5	4	3	2	1

For Double Science the school uses the rule:

GCSE points = Key Stage 3 level − 1

What would be the expected grade for a candidate who gained a level 5 in science at Key Stage 3?

54 In the annual sports day at a school pupils took part in a running race or in a field event or both. Pupils who took part in both were given an award.
In Years 5 and 6 all 72 pupils took part in a running race or in a field event or both.
$\frac{1}{2}$ took part in a running race and $\frac{3}{4}$ took part in a field event.
How many pupils were given an award?

55 A school used the ALIS formula relating predicted A level points scores to mean GCSE points scores for A level mathematics pupils.
The formula used was:

Predicted mathematics A level points score = (mean GCSE points score × 2.24) − 7.35

What was the predicted A level points score for a pupil with a mean GCSE points score of 7.55? Give your answer correct to one decimal place.

56 A teacher compared performance at GCSE with performance at Key Stage 3. The teacher used the following table to convert GCSE grades to points:

Grade	A^*	A	B	C	D	E	F	G
Points	8	7	6	5	4	3	2	1

The formula the teacher used to predict GCSE points was:

GCSE points = 1.2 × Key Stage 3 level − 2

What would be the expected grade for a pupil who gained a level 5 at Key Stage 3?

57 Using the same conversion table and the same formula as in the previous question, what was the likely level at Key Stage 3 for a pupil who gained a grade B at GCSE?

58 There were 27 pupils in a Year 8 history class.
One pupil was absent when there was a mid-term test.
The mean score for the group was 56.
On returning to school the pupil who had been absent took the test and scored 86.
What was the revised mean test score?
Give your answer correct to one decimal place.

59 Teachers in a primary school studied the achievement of pupils over a four-year period. End of Key Stage 2 test results of pupils at the school are given in the table below.

Year	Number of Pupils		
	Level 3	Level 4	Level 5
1997	10	60	18
1998	45	60	25
1999	54	48	26
2000	38	58	24

In what year was the ratio of the combined level 3 and level 4 results to the level 5 results exactly 4 : 1?

60 For a GCSE subject, 20% of the marks were allocated to coursework and 80% to the final examination. The coursework was marked out of 50 and the exam out of 150. A pupil scored 38 for coursework and 112 for the examination.

What was the pupil's final percentage mark for the examination?

Give your answer to the nearest whole number.

4 Interpreting and using statistical information

Notes

Some terms, concepts and forms of representation which are used in statistics may be unfamiliar. The following notes are intended to give a brief summary of some of the unfamiliar aspects.

Some of the information received by schools, e.g. analyses of pupil performance, uses 'cumulative frequencies' or 'cumulative percentages'. One way to illustrate cumulative frequencies is through an example. The table shows the marks gained in a test by the 60 pupils in a year group:

22	13	33	31	51	24	37	83	39	28
31	64	23	35	9	34	42	26	68	38
63	34	44	77	37	15	38	54	34	22
47	25	48	38	53	52	35	45	32	31
37	43	37	49	24	17	48	29	57	33
30	36	42	36	43	38	39	48	39	59

We could complete a tally chart and a frequency table:

Mark, m	Tally	Frequency
9	1	1
10	0	0
11	0	0
12	0	0
13	1	1
and so on		

But 60 results are a lot to analyse and we could group the results together in intervals. A sensible interval in this case would be a band of 10 marks. This is a bit like putting the results into 'bins':

	13	22	33		
		24	31, 37		
		28	39,		
$0 \leqslant m < 10$	$10 \leqslant m < 20$	$20 \leqslant m < 30$	$30 \leqslant m < 40$	$40 \leqslant m < 50$	etc.

Note that $\leqslant$ means 'less than or equal to' and $<$ means 'less than', so $30 \leqslant m < 40$ means all the marks between 30 and 40 including 30 but excluding 40.

Here are the marks grouped into a frequency table:

Mark, m	Frequency	Cumulative frequency
$0 \leqslant m < 10$	1	1
$10 \leqslant m < 20$	3	4
$20 \leqslant m < 30$	9	13
$30 \leqslant m < 40$	25	38
$40 \leqslant m < 50$	11	49
$50 \leqslant m < 60$	6	55
$60 \leqslant m < 70$	3	58
$70 \leqslant m < 80$	1	59
$80 \leqslant m < 90$	1	60

note how the cumulative frequency is calculated:
$\leftarrow 38 = 1 + 3 + 9 + 25$

The last column 'Cumulative frequency' gives the 'running total' – in this case the number of pupils with less than a certain mark. For example, there are 38 pupils who gained less than 40 marks.

The values for cumulative frequency can be plotted to give a cumulative frequency curve as shown below.

Note that the cumulative frequency values are plotted at the right hand end of each interval, i.e. at 10, 20, 30 and so on.

You can use a cumulative frequency curve to estimate the median mark: the median for any particular assessment is the score or level for which half the relevant pupils achieved a higher result and half achieved a lower result.

There are 60 pupils, so the median mark will be the 30th mark. (Find 30 on the vertical scale and go across the graph until you reach the curve and read off the value on the horizontal scale.) The median mark is about 37 – check you agree.

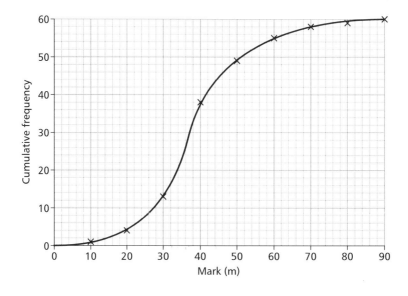

It is also possible to find the quartiles. These were described in the introduction on page 3.

The lower quartile will be at 25% of 60, that is the 15th value, giving a mark of about 31; the upper quartile is at 75% of 60, thus the 45th value, giving a mark of about 45.

The diagram below should further help to explain these terms. It also helps to introduce the idea of a 'box and whisker' plot.

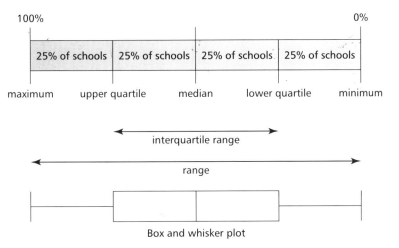

The 'whiskers' indicate the maximum and minimum values, the ends of the 'box' the upper quartile and the lower quartile, and the median is shown by the line drawn across the box.

The 'middle 50%' of the values lie within the box and only the top 25% and the bottom 25% are outside the box. If the ends of the box are close together, then:

● the upper and lower quartiles are close i.e. the interquartile range (that is the difference between them) is small;
● the slope of the cumulative frequency curve (or line) will be steep.

If the ends of the box are not close, then:

● the interquartile range is greater;
● the data is more 'spread out';
● the slope of the curve is less steep.

You need to interpret 'percentile' correctly: the 95th percentile does not mean the mark that 95% of the pupils scored but that 95% of the pupils gained that mark or lower – it is better perhaps to think that only 5% achieved a higher mark.

The use of percentiles is shown in this table:

Comparing a Schools' Performance with National Benchmarks, Average NC levels

example

Percentile	95th	Upper quartile		60th	40th		Lower quartile		5th
English	4.26	4.1	**3.89**	3.89	3.78		3.56		3.36
Mathematics	4.25	3.92		3.85	3.63	**3.63**	3.59		3.24
Science	4.38	4.16		3.91	3.93		3.70	**3.54**	3.49

The figures in bold represent a particular school's average performance.

This table shows, for example, that 5% of pupils nationally gained higher than an average level of 4.26 in the English tests and that 40% of pupils nationally gained an average level of 3.63 or less in mathematics. In other words 60% gained a level higher than 3.63.

The table also shows that the school's performance in English was above average (the 50th percentile) and in line with the 60th percentile, below average in mathematics and well below in science.

questions

1 A secondary school has compared performance on the Key Stage 2 national tests with performance at GCSE. The comparison is shown on the graph below.

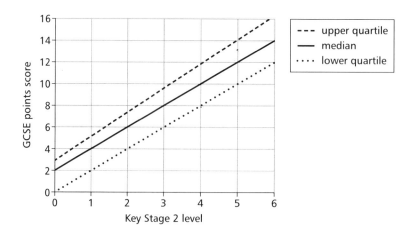

(a) What is the median GCSE points score of those pupils scoring a 2 at Key Stage 2?

(b) A pupil had a Key Stage 2 score of 5 and a GCSE points score of 11. Is it true to say that he was likely to be within the bottom 25% of all pupils?

(c) Is it true that 50% of the pupils who gained level 4 at Key Stage 2 gained GCSE points scores within the range 8 to 12?

2 A teacher produced the following graph to compare performance between the 1999 Key Stage 3 national test results and the 2001 GCSE examinations.

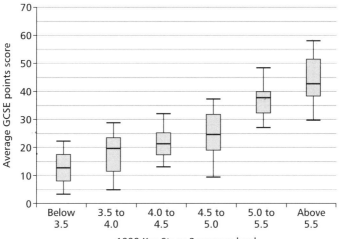

Indicate all the true statements:

1 The median GCSE points score for schools whose average Key Stage 3 level was 5.0–5.5 was 48.

2 50% of schools whose average Key Stage 3 level was 4.0–4.5 achieved average GCSE points scores of between 17 and 25.

3 The range of average GCSE points scores achieved by schools whose average Key Stage 3 level was above 5.5 was about 28.

3 A German language teacher compared the results of a German oral test and a German written test given to a group of 16 pupils.

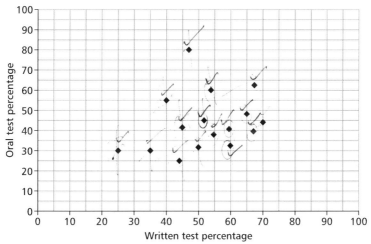

Indicate all the true statements:

1 The range of marks for the oral test is greater than for the written test.

2 $\frac{1}{4}$ of pupils achieved a higher mark on the oral test than on the written test.

3 The two pupils with the lowest marks on the written test also gained the lowest marks on the oral test.

4 A teacher compared the results of an English test taken by all Year 8 pupils.

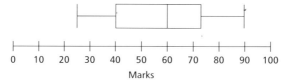

Marks

Indicate all the true statements:

1 $\frac{1}{4}$ of all the pupils scored more than 70 marks.
2 $\frac{1}{2}$ of all pupils scored less than 60 marks.
3 The range of marks was 65.

5 In 1998 a survey was made of the nightly TV viewing habits of 10-year-old children in town A and town B. The findings are shown in the pie charts below:

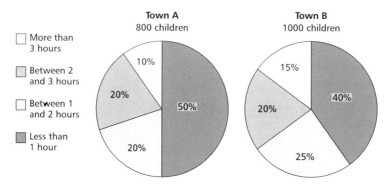

Use these pie charts to identify which of the following statements is true:

1 More children in town A watched TV for less than 1 hour than in town B.
2 More children in town B watched for between 2 and 3 hours than in town A.
3 100 children watched more than 3 hours in town A.

6 This bar chart shows a comparison between England, Scotland, Northern Ireland and Wales in the percentage participation in higher education by young people.

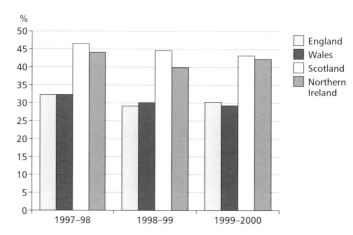

Indicate all the true statements:

1 In all 4 countries the percentage of young people participating increases between 1997–8 and 1999–2000.
2 Between 1997–8 and 1999–2000 there was approximately a change of 2 percentage points in the numbers for Northern Ireland.
3 England was the only country to see an increase between 1998–9 and 1999–2000.

7 At the beginning of Year 11 pupils at a school took an internal test which was used to predict GCSE grades in mathematics. From the results the predicted grades were plotted on a cumulative frequency graph.

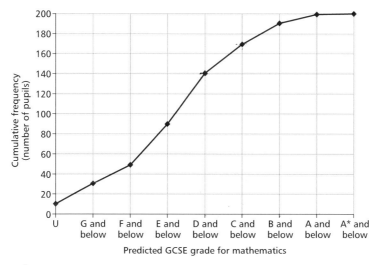

Indicate the true statement:

1 30% of the pupils were predicted to achieve grade C.
2 85% of the pupils were predicted to achieve grade C.
3 15% of the pupils were predicted to achieve grade C.

8 This bar chart shows the amount of pocket money children in Year 7 receive:

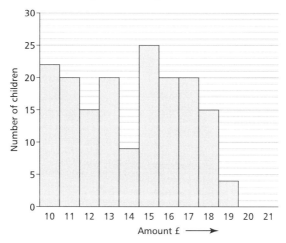

(a) How many children were surveyed?

(b) What is the modal amount of pocket money received?

9 The mean height of 20 girls in Year 7 is 1.51 m. Another girl who is 1.6 m joins the class. Calculate the new mean height.

10 A Year 7 teacher was given information from feeder primary schools about pupils in the tutor group.

The two box plots below show the reading scores for two feeder schools A and B.

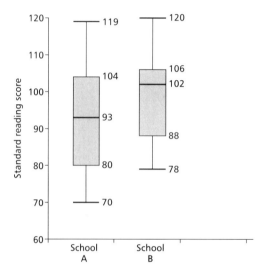

A standard reading score of 100 shows that a pupil's reading score was exactly on the national average for pupils of the same age. Standard scores of more than 100 show above average reading scores and below 100 show below average reading scores for pupils of the same age.
Indicate all the true statements:

1 The difference in the median scores for the two feeder schools was 9.

2 The interquartile range of the scores for school B was 18.

3 The range of scores was 9 less for school B than for school A.

11 Use the box plots and the information from question 10 to indicate the true statements:

1 50% of the pupils in school A had a reading score of 93 or more.

2 25% of pupils in school B scored 88 or less.

3 The interquartile range for the two schools was the same.

12 The following bar chart shows the number of Year 12 pupils on GNVQ courses in 1999 and 2000.

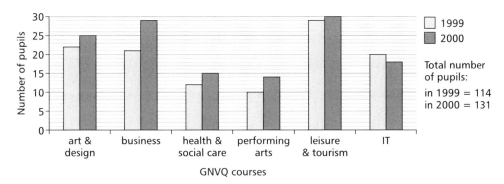

By how many percentage points had the number of Year 12 pupils on the GNVQ leisure and tourism course changed between 1999 and 2000 when compared with the total number of GNVQ pupils for each year?

Give your answer to one decimal place.

13 This box and whisker graph shows the relationship between Key Stage 3 English tests and the scores in a school's test.

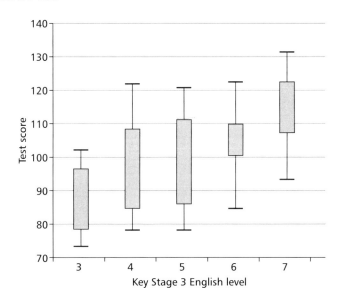

Estimate the range of test scores achieved by the middle 50% of students who gained a level 5 at Key Stage 3.

14 This box and whisker diagram shows the GCSE results for 4 subjects for a school in 2002.

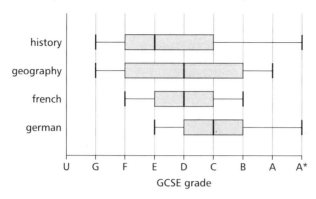

Indicate all the true statements:

1 50% of the pupils who took history gained grades F to C.
2 French had the lowest median grade.
3 50% of the pupils who took German gained grades C to A*.

15 The marks of ten students in the two papers of a German examination were plotted on this scatter graph:

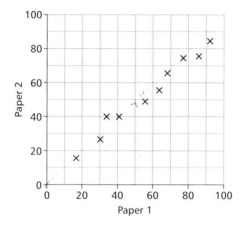

A student scored 53 marks on Paper 1 but missed Paper 2. What would you estimate her mark to be on Paper 2?

16 The graph shows GCSE total points scores compared with end of Key Stage 3 assessment mean level. The line is the national median line. The points A, B, C, D show the achievement of four pupils.

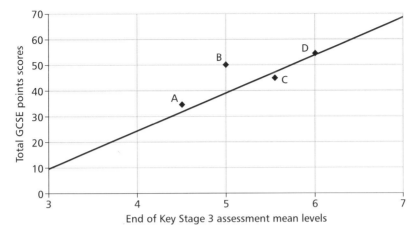

End of Key Stage 3 assessment mean levels

Indicate all the true statements:

1 Pupil D achieved as well as might have been predicted at GCSE.
2 Pupil C achieved a higher level at end of Key Stage 3 than Pupil B but scored fewer points at GCSE than Pupil B.
3 At GCSE Pupil B achieved better than might have been predicted but Pupil A achieved less well than might have been predicted.

17 A teacher compared pupil performance in reading in the Key Stage 1 national tests:

Level achieved	Sex	Year	Percentage of Pupils	
			School	*National*
2 and above	All	1997	81.8	79.5
2 and above	All	1998	82.3	79.0
2 and above	All	1999	83.4	81.1
2 and above	All	2000	83.6	81.1
2 and above	Boys	1997	78.4	73.9
2 and above	Boys	1998	77.6	74.2
2 and above	Boys	1999	79.0	76.7
2 and above	Boys	2000	79.0	76.4
2 and above	Girls	1997	85.3	84.3
2 and above	Girls	1998	87.1	84.0
2 and above	Girls	1999	88.2	85.7
2 and above	Girls	2000	88.4	85.8

Indicate all the true statements:

1 The performance for the school is consistently above the national average.
2 Girls out perform boys in the reading tests in the school.
3 The percentage of boys achieving level 2 and above increased annually in the school.

18 20 pupils in a class took Test A at the beginning of a term and Test B at the end of the term.

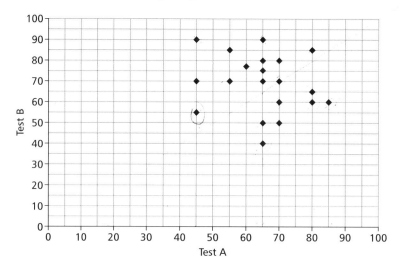

Indicate all the true statements:

1 The range of marks was wider for Test A than for Test B.

2 The lowest mark in Test A was lower than the lowest mark in Test B.

3 40% of the pupils scored the same mark or lower in Test B than in Test A.

4 More pupils scored over 60% in test A than in test B.

19 A teacher analysed the reading test standardised scores of a group of pupils:

Pupil	Gender	Age 8+ test standardised score	Age 10+ test standardised score
A	F	100	108
B	M	78	89
C	M	88	92
D	M	110	102
E	F	102	110
F	F	88	84
G	M	119	128
H	F	80	84

Indicate all the true statements:

1 All the girls improved their standardised scores between the Age 8+ and the Age 10+ tests.

2 The greatest improvement between the Age 8+ and the Age 10+ tests was achieved by a boy.

3 $\frac{1}{4}$ of all the pupils had lower standardised scores in the Age 10+ tests than in the Age 8+ tests.

20 The graph shows the predicted achievements of pupils in English at the end of Key Stage 3 based on the results of tests taken at the beginning of Year 9.

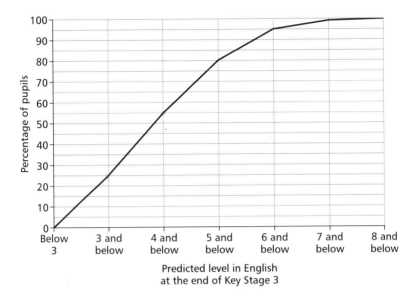

What percentage of pupils was predicted to achieve level 4 and above?

5 Answers and key points

Key knowledge

1   (a) 4.3   (b) 4.44   (c) 10.09   (d) 5.4   (e) 1.48   (f) 9.19

> **Key point**
> Remember to line up the decimal points.

2   (a) 42   (b) 0.35   (c) 2

3   (a) $\frac{2}{100} = \frac{1}{50}$ (b) $\frac{25}{100} = \frac{1}{4}$ (c) $\frac{85}{100} = \frac{17}{20}$ (d) $\frac{12.5}{100} = \frac{1}{8}$ (e) $\frac{47}{100}$

> **Key point**
> Cancel down by dividing both numerator and denominator by the same factor.

4   (a) $\frac{3}{8} \times \frac{100\%}{1} = 3 \times 12.5\% = 37.5\%$ (b) $\frac{13}{25} \times \frac{100\%}{1} = 52\%$

     (c) $\frac{12}{40} \times \frac{100\%}{1} = \frac{3}{10} \times \frac{100\%}{1} = 30\%$ (d) $\frac{36}{60} \times \frac{100\%}{1} = \frac{6}{10} \times \frac{100\%}{1} = 60\%$

> **Key point**
> There are different ways of simplifying – which way is best depends on the numbers in the question, but if the denominator is a multiple of 10, it is probably easier to try to cancel down to get 10, as in (c) and (d), unless you are using a calculator in which case change the fraction into a decimal then multiply by 100.

5   (a) $0.25 \times £40 = £10$ (b) $0.75 \times £20 = £15$ (c) $0.12 \times 5 = 6$ (d) $0.2 \times 45 = 9$

> **Key point**
> Change each percentage into a decimal.

6   (a) $\frac{2}{3}$ divide by 12, or by 2, then 2 then 3   (b) $\frac{3}{5}$ divide by 6

     (c) $\frac{2}{5}$ divide by 15, or by 3, then 5   (d) $\frac{3}{4}$ divide by 25

7 $\frac{39}{60}$

> **Key point**
> Change each fraction to a decimal.

8   Girls:

mean	= 50 (to the nearest whole number)
median	= 48
mode	= 48
range	= 63 – 45 = 18

For both boys and girls the median, mode and range are the same but the mean for the girls is slightly higher so one could deduce that the girls are slightly better than the boys, but the difference is not significant.

Key point
Make sure you put the values in order before finding the median. See the working out for the boys if you have any difficulties.

Mental arithmetic

(1) 55 minutes

Key point
Count on from 1 hour 20

(2) 28

Key point
70% of 40 = 0.7 × 40 or $\frac{7}{10}$ × 40

(3) 17

Key point
Note 100 ÷ 6 = 16.666 therefore 17

(4) 450

Key point
Quicker to calculate $\frac{3}{4}$ of 600 than find $\frac{1}{4}$ of 600 and subtract.

(5) 9

Key point
Note 450 ÷ 52 = 8.65 therefore 9

(6) 48

Key point
Calculate as 30 ÷ 5 = 6, then 6 × 8 = 48 or 8 ÷ 5 = 1.6 so 30 × 1.6 = 3 × 16 = 48

(7) 12:40

Key point
Count on 1 hr 10 minutes + 2 hours.

(8) 11

Key point
10 rows for 400 people, so one more row needed for the remaining 32

9 84%

Key point
21 hours remaining $= \frac{21}{25} = 84\%$

10 11.10 am

Key point
Video + tidying needs 25 + 10 = 35 mins, so 11.45 − 35 = 11.10

11 8

Key point
Remember: to convert fractions with denominators of 25 to a percentage, multiply the numerator by 4: $\frac{22}{25} = 88\%$, therefore 8% difference.

12 £500

Key point
Simplify quickly by changing into £: 200 × 50 × 5p = £2 × 50 × 5

13 60%

Key point
Common factor is 7, therefore $\frac{42}{70} = \frac{6}{10} = 60\%$

14 720p or £7.20

Key point
Work out as 120 × 2 × 3 = 120 × 6

15 0.075

Key point
Think of $7\frac{1}{2}\%$ as 7.5% then divide by 100

16 15

Key point
Work out as $\frac{3}{7} \times 35$

17 265

Key point
(5 × 25) + (5 × 28)

18 22 hours and 5 minutes

Key point
5 × (4 hr 25 mins) = (5 × 4 hr) + (5 × 25 min) = 20 hr + 125 mins = 20 hr + 2 hr 5 mins

19 3

> **Key point**
> Find 1% of 300

20 14

> **Key point**
> Think of the context: 3 pupils per half hour lesson.
> $\therefore$ 40 ÷ 3 = 13 r 1 so 14 half hour periods.

21 1 hr 10 mins

> **Key point**
> The calculation is 3 hr – 1 hr 50 mins.

22 18

> **Key point**
> Find 60% of 30

23 6.25 m^2

> **Key point**
> The calculation is 2.5 × 2.5. You should know what 25^2 is.

24 12

> **Key point**
> Quicker to find 40% or 0.4 × 30 = 12

25 95

> **Key point**
> Quicker to find 10% or 0.1 × 950 = 95

26 63

> **Key point**
> The calculation is 0.2 × 315 = 63

27 20

> **Key point**
> Quicker to find $\frac{1}{8}$ and then five eighths by multiplying by 5

28 56%

> **Key point**
> With 25 as the denominator you should know that you multiply the numerator by 4

29   14

Key point
Find $\frac{1}{5}$ and double to give $\frac{2}{5} \times 35 = 14$

30   76%

Key point
$\frac{19}{25}$ – multiply 19 by 4 to get the %

31   0.125

Key point
Write it as a fraction and divide by 100.

32   405.6

Key point
Simple to multiply by 100 but be careful!

General arithmetic

1   Mean = 29.7; mode = 24; range = 17

Key point
$$\text{Mean} = \frac{33 \times 2 + 29 \times 5 + 34 \times 5 + 36 \times 7 + 19 \times 2 + 24 \times 8 + 27 \times 1}{30} = \frac{890}{30} = 29.7$$
Mode = most frequent mark, not the number of times it occurs.

2   £2.53

Key point
100 euros = $£\frac{100}{1.43}$ = £69.93 and 100 euros = $£\frac{100}{1.38}$ = £72.46

3   5 gained level 3

Key point
If 2 gained level 1 then 30 gained either level 2 or level 3. The ratio of level 2 numbers to level 3 numbers is 5 to 1. Divide 30 by (5 + 1), i.e. into 6 equal groups so each group has 5 pupils so 25 pupils gained level 2 and 5 gained level 3.

4   School A

Key point
Percentages are: School A = 66.7%; school B = 65.6%; school C = 65.7%

5 10 below.

Key point
Find 18% of 250 = 0.18 × 250 = 45, so 10 below.

6 Answer number 3; 65%

Key point
For coursework the mark, as a percentage, $= \frac{22}{40} \times 100\% = 55\%$
For the exam the mark, as a percentage $= \frac{135}{200} \times 100\% = 67.5\%$
Coursework contributes 20% or $\frac{1}{5}$ to the final mark = 0.2 × 55% or $\frac{1}{5}$ × 55% = 11%
The exam contributes 80% or $\frac{4}{5}$ to the final mark = 0.8 × 67.5% or $\frac{4}{5}$ × 67.5% = 54%
The final mark = 11% + 54% = 65%, so answer = 3

7 (a) 69   (b) 39.1%   (c) 55%   (d) 53%

Key point
You need to read tables carefully and decide whether or when you need to calculate in columns or in rows.
(a)   Total swimmers = 27 + 42 = 69
(b)   Percentage of girl swimmers = $\frac{27}{69}$ × 100% = 39.1%
(c)   Total girls = 27 + 33 = 60
      % of girls $\frac{33}{60}$ = × 100% = 55%
(d)   Total students = 27 + 33 + 42 + 28 = 130
      % swimmers = $\frac{69}{130}$ × 100% = 53.1%

8 A

Key point
The calculation is $\left(\frac{58}{75} \times 0.6\right) + \left(\frac{65}{125} \times 0.4\right) = 0.464 + 0.208 = 0.672$ ie 67.2%

9 3

Key point
Convert to percentages.

10 39%

Key point
Total number of pupils = 16 + 34 + 30 + 42 + 35 + 27 + 16 = 200
Pupils with 60 marks or more = 35 + 27 + 16 = 78

11 English A*   Mathematics B   Science D

Key point
You need to read both question and table carefully.

12 339

Key point
Take 5% off the total of 357 i.e. $0.95 \times 357 = 339.15$, but round up to 340 because 339 would be $\frac{1}{2}$ day too few.

13 (a) 53.4° (b) class 6B

Key point
Easy to make mistakes by confusing 'year group' and 'class'.
Total for each class: class A = 30 pupils, class B = 28 pupils
Total for year = 58 pupils
(a) Total pupils gaining level 4 or better = $11 + 5 + 14 + 1 = 31$
As a percentage = $\frac{31}{58} \times 100\% = 53.4\%$
(b) In class A the percentage = $\frac{16}{30} \times 100\% = 53.3\%$
in class B the percentage = $\frac{15}{28} \times 100\% = 53.5\%$, therefore answer is class B

14 School Q

Key point
Change each figure into decimals:
$\frac{2}{9} = 0.222$ 57 out of 300 = 0.19   18% = 0.18

15 7

Key point
Look at table 2. To miss level 4 by 1 level thus gaining level 3 means you need to identify pupils scoring marks between 25 and 51.

16 4.5

Key point
Use a ruler to help – find 6 on the horizontal axis and read off the corresponding value on the vertical axis.

17 28%

Key point
Because the times both involve half-hours, it is simply working out $\frac{6.5}{23.5}$ $\times 100\% = 27.66\% = 28\%$ to the nearest per cent.

18 50%

Key point
Subtract, remembering 12 months in a year. Pupils A, C, E, G, H fit the criteria.

19 $\frac{35}{60} = \frac{7}{12}$

Key point
Count pupil numbers carefully – jot down totals.

20   15

Key point
$1500 \div 100 = 15$

21   a

Key point
Number of 'pupil laps' = $(65 \times 8 + 94 \times 10) = 1460$.
Total distance = $1460 \times 700 = 1\ 022\ 000$ metres = 1022 km

22   10

Key point
Use a sketch – 3 small sheets per width of large sheet.

23   1409

Key point
Remember last pupil doesn't need 2 minutes changeover time.

24   3.75 m^2

Key point
$2.5 \times 1.5 = 3.75$ m^2

25   (a) 192 km   (b) 31 miles (actually 31.25)

Key point
The calculations are: (a) $120 \times \frac{8}{5}$ (b) $50 \times \frac{5}{8}$

26   0.1 mm

Key point
Take care with the units – work in millimetres i.e. $50 \div 500$.

27   55

Key point
Don't 'double count' the top corner slab.

28   128 cm

Key point
You can fit 8 lots of 15 cm across the 120 cm width.

29   5.30 am

Key point
Remember time = distance ÷ speed. The travel time = $120 \div 40 = 3$ hr. Add 0.5 hour, therefore total time = 3.5 hours.

30 16 km

Key point
Total map distance = 32.3 cm = 32.3 × 50 000 cm on the ground = 16.15 km

31 363.6 seconds = 6 minutes 3.6 seconds.

Key point
Add up the time in seconds and decimals of seconds giving 363.6 seconds then convert.

32 £65.88; £83.88

Key point
Remember to work in £ on the mileage rate.

33 28 pupils.

Key point
From 9.00 to 10.30 is 90 minutes → she can see 4 pupils.
From 10.45 to 12.00 is 75 minutes → she can see 3 pupils.
Total for the day = 7 pupils, total over 4 days = 28 pupils.
If the calculations were done using the total figures:
   her working week = 4 × 3 hours less 4 × 15 minutes = 11 hours
   11 hours = 660 minutes ÷ 20, giving 33 pupils
This would be incorrect because it ignores the 'structure' of the school morning.

34 43.2 km

Key point
1 cm = 6 km, therefore 7.2 cm = 7.2 × 6 km

35 8.1 m

Key point
The fact that 250 parents are coming is redundant information. Working in metres the calculation is 2 × 8 × 0.45 + 0.9

36 8 layers.

Key point
The calculation, working in centimetres is 124 ÷ 15 = 8.266, so round down.

37 61 minutes.

Key point
The calculation is 15 + 4 × 10 + 3 × 2

20   15

38 11 : 20

> **Key point**
> 400 km = 250 miles

39 36.5

> **Key point**
> Revised mark = 50 × 0.8 − 3.5 = 36.5

40 25

> **Key point**
> Sample size = 10 + 150 ÷ 10 = 25

41 82.2 °C

> **Key point**
> Remember to work out the brackets first:
> $$C = \frac{5(180 - 32)}{9} = \frac{5 \times 148}{9} = 82.2$$

42 20 °C

> **Key point**
> Remember to work out the brackets first:
> $$C = \frac{5(68 + 40)}{9} - 40 = \frac{5 \times 108}{9} - 40 = 20$$

43 72

> **Key point**
> Remember to work out brackets first and to round up.

44 55

> **Key point**
> You can check the method by working through the data for pupil A.
> The calculation for pupil E is $\frac{18}{30} \times 0.25 + \frac{64}{120} \times 0.75 = 0.15 + 0.4 = 0.55 = 55\%$

45 (b) (c)

> **Key point**
> Greatest range is test 5 (92 − 15 = 77)

46 53

> **Key point**
> The calculation is 64 × 0.6 + 36 × 0.3 + 40 × 0.1 = 53.2, i.e. 53

47 30

> **Key point**
> The calculation is $80 \times 0.6 + M \times 0.4 = 60$ so $M \times 0.4 = 60 - 48 = 12$.
> Therefore $M = \frac{12}{0.4} = 30$

48 24

> **Key point**
> Total possible score = 120. 70% of 120 = 84. Therefore marks should add to 84.
> Therefore test 4 mark = 24. OR mean score of 70% = $\frac{21}{30}$. Therefore total
> marks = $4 \times 21 = 84$ so test 4 mark is 24

49 7.5 km/h

> **Key point**
> Speed = distance ÷ time = $6 \div 0.8$ (NB. work in hours, 48 mins = $\frac{4}{5}$ hr = 0.8 hr)

50 23.67

> **Key point**
> You must work out $20 \div 15$ first, not $25 - 20$ then divide by 15.
> Therefore reading level = $5 + (20 - 1.33) = 5 + 18.67 = 23.67$

51 5.51

> **Key point**
> The total points are given by $(4 \times 5) + (4 \times 6) + (1 \times 7) + (1 \times 8) = 59$
> The calculation is then $(\frac{59}{10} \times 3.9) - 17.5 = 5.51$

52 87

> **Key point**
> The calculation is $\quad 80 = A \times 0.6 + 70 \times 0.4$
> $\qquad\qquad\qquad\qquad 80 = A \times 0.6 + 28$
> Therefore $\qquad\qquad A \times 0.6 = 52$
> $\qquad\qquad\qquad\qquad A = 52 \div 0.6 = 86.67$, i.e. 87

53 Grade D

> **Key point**
> The calculation is: GCSE points = $5 - 1 = 4$. Therefore Grade = D

54 18

> **Key point**
> $\frac{3}{4} - \frac{1}{2} = \frac{1}{4}$ so $\frac{1}{4}$ receive a merit.

55 9.6

Key point
Work out brackets first.

56 Grade D

Key point
The points are given by $1.2 \times 5 - 2 = 4$; therefore, from the table, 4 points = Grade D

57 Level 7

Key point
From the table a Grade B gives 6 points.
The calculation is $6 = 1.2 \times L - 2$. Thus $1.2 \times L = 8$ and $L = 6.66$, i.e. level 7

58 57.1

Key point
Total for 2̶6̶ pupils = 2̶6̶ × 56 = 1512. New total = 1512 + 86 = 1598
New mean = 1598 ÷ 2̶7̶

(handwritten: 1456   1456   1542)
(handwritten: 1542 . 57.1)
(handwritten: 1542)

59 2000

Key point
Multiplying each level 5 score by 4 should help identify the year.

60 75%

Key point
Find 20% of $\frac{38}{50}$ = 15.2% and find 80% of $\frac{112}{150}$ = 59.7% total = 74.9%

Interpreting and using statistical information

1 (a) 6   (b) No   (c) Yes

Key points
1 (a) Find 2 on the KS2 axis and move up the graph until you reach the median line.
        Read off the value on the GCSE axis.
   (b) Find 12 on the GCSE axis and 5 on the KS2 axis. The lines through these values
        intersect in the space between the lower quartile line and the median line so
        it is not true – remember that 25% of the pupils are below the lower quartile.
   (c) Find 4 on the KS2 axis, 50% will lie between 8 (the lower quartile) and 12 (the
        upper quartile).

2 2 and 3 are true

Key point
1 the median is the line inside the 'box'; 2 50% is represented by the box 3
range = highest – lowest = 58 – 30 = 28

3 1 and 2 are true

Key point
1 oral range = 80 − 25 = 55; written range = 70 − 25 = 45; 2 imagine a line drawn from (0, 0) to (100, 100). This is the line where scores on both tests were the same. There are 4 points above this line, $\frac{4}{16} = \frac{1}{4}$
3 lowest written marks are 25 and 35 scoring 30 in the oral but one pupil scored 25 in the oral.

4 2 and 3 are true

Key point
1 the upper quartile is at 73 not 70; 2 median is at 60 so true; 3 range = 90 − 25 = 65 so true.

5 Only 2 is true

Key points
It is important to realise that, although the pie charts appear to be the same size, they represent different 'quantities' – 800 children and 1000 children.
Statement 1: is not true. 50% of 800 = 40% of 1000. (0.5 × 800 = 400 and 0.4 × 1000 = 400)
Statement 2: is true. 20% of 1000 is more than 20% of 800 (0.2 × 1000 = 200, 0.2 × 800 = 160)
Statement 3: is not true.10% of 800 = 80

6 Only 2 is true

Key point
1 obvious – e.g. 1999–2000 columns lower than 1997–8; 2 1997–8 NI value is about 44 and 42 in 1999–2000; 3 NI also increases.

7 Only 3 is true

Key point
140 pupils get D and below, 170 get C and below so 30 get grade C.

8 (a) 170 (b) £15

Key point
(a) Add up the values given by the tops of each bar:
    22 + 20 + 15 + 20 + 9 + 25 + 20 + 20 + 15 + 4
(b) The modal amount is that received by the most children, i.e. £15 received by 25 children.

9   1.514 m

Key point
The total height for the 20 girls = 20 × 1.51 = 30.2 m
The new total height = 30.2 + 1.6 = 31.8 m but this is for 21 girls.
The new mean height = 31.8 ÷ 21 = 1.514 m

10   1 and 2 are true

Key point
1 medians are 102 and 93; 2 interquartile range for B = 106 − 88; 3 school A
range = 119 − 70, school B range = 120 − 78

11   1 and 2 are true

Key point
1 50% lie above the median line; 2 25% lie below the lower quartile; 3 IQ range for
A = 24 and for B = 18

12   2.5%

Key point
Total for 1999 = 114, and for 2000 = 131 − given in question.
1999 tourism number = 29 and $\frac{29}{114}$ = 25.4%
2000 number = 30 and $\frac{30}{131}$ = 22.9%

13   About 25

Key point
Using the box and whisker diagram corresponding to level 5, the scores of the
middle 50%, are given by the upper and lower ends of the box i.e. about
111 − 86 = 25.

14   1 and 3 are true

Key point
1 history 'box' extends from F to C; 2 history has a lower median grade 3 German
median is at grade C so 50% gained C to A*

15   About 45–49 marks

Key point
You need to draw in the line of best fit through the points.

16   1 and 2 are true

Key point
1 D lies on the line; 2 C is to the right of but below B; 3 A is above the line so A also
achieved better than might have been predicted.

17 1 and 2 are true

Key point
1 Check the school numbers are always greater than the national figures.
2 Check the girls numbers are always greater than the boys.
3 Decreased in 1998.

18 3 and 4 are true

Key point
1 Range for A = 85 − 45 = 40, range for B = 90 − 40 = 50.
2 Lowest value for A = 45 and for B = 40.
3 Imagine a line drawn from (0, 0) to (100, 100) 8 pupils on or below the line and
$\frac{8}{40}$ = 40%
4 14 scored *over* 60% in A and 13 scored *over* 60% in B.

19 2 and 3 are true

Key point
1 Pupil F score decreased; 2 Pupil B score increased by 11; 3 2 pupils, (D, F) had lower scores.

20 75%

Key point
25% gained level 3 and below so 75% gained more than level 3 i.e. level 4 and above.